I LIKE BEING IN PARISH MINISTRY

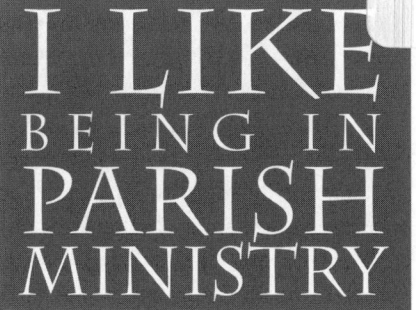

Catechist

Alison Berger

TWENTY-THIRD PUBLICATIONS

185 WILLOW STREET • PO BOX 180 • MYSTIC, CT 06355
TEL: 1-800-321-0411 • FAX: 1-800-572-0788
E-MAIL: ttpubs@aol.com • www.twentythirdpublications.com

Twenty-Third Publications
A Division of Bayard
185 Willow Street
P.O. Box 180
Mystic, CT 06355
(860) 536-2611
(800) 321-0411
www.twentythirdpublications.com

ISBN:1-58595-214-1
Printed in the U.S.A.

CONTENTS

INTRODUCTION

I had my first taste of being a catechist when I was ten years old. My sister Geri celebrated her First Communion that year, and I organized my cousins, brother, and sister in a reenactment of the event. We put our presentation together quickly, complete with Mass in Latin (Mass wasn't in the vernacular yet). With my sketchy knowledge of Latin and even sketchier knowledge of theology, I coached the other actors and actresses in their parts: my nine-year-old brother was the priest, my six-year-old cousin the altar server, my nine-year-old cousin played my sister, my five-year-old sister was the "congregation," and I was the nun-teacher. The part I still remember best is the ending, when my "sister" exclaimed to her "teacher," "I'm so happy because I received Jesus today!"

Isn't this what the ministry of catechesis is all about—helping our children, young people, families, single adults develop their personal relationship with Jesus, and through Jesus with God? "The definitive aim of catechesis is to put people not only in touch, but also in intimacy, with Jesus Christ" (*Catechesi Tradendae*, in the *General Directory for Catechesis*, #80).

The word catechesis has its roots in the Greek word "katecheo," which means to resound or echo. In a way each of us is like an instrument on which the Spirit plays the music of God's love for us in Jesus. The music that comes from each of us is unique because it filters through our personalities, our qualities, even our weaknesses.

Growth in our prayer life, formation and instruction in our ministry, and attentiveness to God and to our sisters and brothers will help us keep our instruments carefully tuned so that the music—the gospel message—that God wants to communicate through us will be as authentic and clear as possible: "a living, explicit and fruitful expression of faith" (*General Directory for Catechesis*, #82).

Whether you accompany second graders on the journey of Christian initiation, are part of an RCIA team, teach sixth graders in a Catholic school, coordinate intergenerational activities, or work with youngsters who have special needs, you are a minister of the Word. You hold a privileged and important place in the heart of the Church. You are specialists of the Word, direct witnesses to God's amazing action in human history. In this book I would like to spend some time with you looking at the vocation of the catechist, the qualities, formation, and spirituality of the catechist, as well as some "how-tos."

In preparing this book, I relied on certain key documents such as the *General Directory for Catechesis* (*GDC*), Pope Paul VI's *On Evangelization in Our Time* (*Evangelii Nuntiandi, EN*), and Pope John Paul II's *On Catechesis in Our Time* (*Catechesi Tradendae, CT*). You will find more information about these documents in the Resources section at the end of this book. For reasons of space I'll use the abbreviations included above when giving the citation for any direct quotes or reference

A
VOCATION
AND
MINISTRY

W hen Christ had finished his work on earth, it
is said, and had returned to heaven, the angel
Gabriel met him. "Lord," said Gabriel, "may
I ask what plans you have made for carrying on your work
on earth?" "I have chosen some men and women," said
Christ. "They will pass my message on till it reaches the
whole world." "But," said the angel, "supposing those few
people fail you—what other plans have you made?" Christ
smiled, "I have no other plans," he said. "I am counting on
them."

—Anonymous

God has "counted on" many messengers throughout salvation
history, and has communicated with them in various ways. Saul

the Pharisee, who was to become Paul the apostle, saw a light from heaven while he was traveling to Damascus to imprison the Christians (Acts 9). The prophet Isaiah had a heavenly vision in which the Lord asked, "Whom shall I send?" (Is 6:1–8). But the disciples Peter and Andrew were fishing when Jesus invited them to follow him; James and John were mending their nets, and Matthew was in his tax collector's booth.

God calls people to the ministry of catechist in many different ways, but the calling is always a vocation rooted in the catechist's baptism. Through baptism every Christian shares in the prophetic mission of Christ, to be spokespersons for God. Catechists are spokespersons because they carry out a form of ministry of the Word. The invitation to this ministry might come through another catechist, through a parish leader, through an event that inspires a person to serve others in some way.

Bishops, priests, and catechetical leaders are in the forefront of the ministry of catechesis. There are religious communities whose specific work is to catechetize. But the Church's mission of catechesis depends on individuals who dedicate themselves to sharing their faith in Christ, to helping others discover Christ's presence in their lives. Lay catechists who live and love and work in the world along with those to whom they minister bring a special sensitivity and understanding to their proclamation of and witness to the Word.

Those of us involved in catechetical ministry reflect on our experience of God and strive to share our faith in a way relevant to young people and adults of today. Our baptismal consecration makes our proclamation and witness—our ministry—sacramental, that is, a living sign of Christ's presence. Baptism empowers us to realize the object of catechesis, that is, to lead people—children, youth, adults—to profess their faith in Christ and in the one God.

Of course, we don't do this on our own. The Church commissions us to carry out this ministry in her name. When our parish community appoints us as catechists, it is the Church sending us forth for this ministry of the word. This reality is a source of encouragement and support. We inherit the 2000 years of wisdom and grace that are the fruit of the Church's rich, turbulent, and diverse history. We stand shoulder to shoulder with both sinners and saints. And we can rely on the guidance of the Holy Spirit.

Two personal stories
In the following stories two catechists tell how they became involved in catechesis, and talk about what they receive from their ministry. After reading the stories, use the reflection questions that follow as a springboard for "telling your own story," either in a journal or in a group sharing.

One summer an article appeared in our Sunday bulletin asking for six volunteers to teach preschool and kindergarten in the parish religious education program. At the time my daughter was five years old and full of questions about God. I thought this would be a wonderful experience for both of us. However, I was full of doubt as to whether I was qualified to be a catechist. Over the next five days I was haunted by one question: what if I did not call to volunteer and because of me the parish did not start this program? So I made the call and spent the next ten years as a catechist in preschool, kindergarten, and third grade. Later I became the program secretary.

Working closely with the children, watching them grow in the knowledge of the Lord, seeing their faces light up when they realize they do know what we are trying to teach them—these are the little things that make this ministry so rewarding for me.

—Judy Scanlan
St. Christopher Parish, Midlothian, Illinois

I am pleased and proud to admit this is my seventh year serving as a catechist for St. Eugene's parish. My husband and I have been members here since we were married seventeen years ago. Leaving the working world and a job I loved was a tough adjustment for me when our second child was born. I prayed for an answer to end this struggle and for peace. My prayers were answered when the third grade catechist I was assisting suddenly left the program and I was offered her class. I am thrilled to spread the Lord's Good News each week with our church leaders of tomorrow. My role as catechist is one of those gifts that keeps on giving. I love it!

—Michelle Stephenson
St. Eugene's Catholic Church, Cuyahoga Falls, Ohio

FOR YOUR REFLECTION

• When did you first feel the call to be a catechist? Was your response more like Isaiah's (Here I am; send me), or Moses' (Who am I that I should go to Pharaoh?) or like Jeremiah's (Lord God, truly I do not know how to speak)? Who or what was instrumental in helping you realize and follow your call?

_____

_____

_____

_____

• What does being a catechist mean to you? What do you like best about it? What do you find the hardest?

_____

_____

_____

_____

- Read the story of Moses' call (Ex 3:1–15), or Jeremiah (Jer 1:4-12), or Paul's reflection on his mission (1 Cor 1:17-2:5). All these passages speak of God's promise to be with those whom he calls to the service of the Word. How and when have you experienced God's presence in your ministry?

_____

_____

_____

_____

- What do you hope to gain personally from your ministry as a catechist?

_____

_____

_____

_____

_____

_____

_____

_____

_____

_____

_____

_____

_____

Let these words lead you to prayer.

Therefore, since it is by God's mercy that we are engaged in this ministry, we do not lose heart. We have renounced the shameful things that one hides; we refuse to practice cunning or to falsify God's word; but by the open statement of the truth we commend ourselves to the conscience of everyone in the sight of God.…For we do not proclaim ourselves; we proclaim Jesus Christ as Lord and ourselves as your slaves for Jesus' sake. For it is the God who said, "Let light shine out of darkness," who has shone in our hearts to give the light of the knowledge of the glory of God in the face of Jesus Christ.

—2 Corinthians 4:1–2, 5–6

THE OBJECT OF CATECHESIS

In the mountainous regions of North India, where it is very cold, travelers keep warm in this way. They take a small vessel, put burning coal in it, and cover it up. They weave strings around it and, wrapping it with cloth, carry it under their arms.

Now, three men were traveling this way one evening, when one of them saw several other travelers suffering from the cold. Taking the fire out of his vessel, he lit a fire so everyone could get warm. When it grew dark, the second man took out the fire in his vessel and lit a torch with it and helped everyone walk in safety.

The third man mocked the other two and said, "You are fools. You have wasted your fire for the sake of others."

"Show us your fire," they said to him. When he broke

open his vessel, there was no fire, only ashes and coal. With their fire one man had given warmth and another had given light, but the third was selfish and the fire was of no use even to him.

In the same way, it is God's will that the fire of the Holy Spirit we receive should give warmth and light to others.

—Sadhu Sindar Singh

We catechists must share the fire. The object of catechesis is communion with Jesus Christ, to help those who have been baptized in Christ to know him better, to know his mystery, to know the kingdom of God, and the "paths he has laid down for anyone who wishes to follow him" (*General Directory for Catechesis*, #80). Through this communion with Jesus Christ we are, in turn, united with God his Father and God the Holy Spirit, and with the Church, Christ's body. We share with others the fire of love, the Holy Spirit.

How is this communion with Christ realized? At the end of his earthly life Jesus responded to a question from his disciple Thomas: "Lord, we do not know where you are going. How can we know the way?" Jesus answered, "I am the way, and the truth, and the life. No one comes to the Father except through me" (Jn 14:5–6).

The way to communion with Christ is to know, to celebrate, to live, and to contemplate the mystery of Jesus Christ (*GDC*, #84). And as we accompany those to whom we minister on this journey, we as catechists need to make that journey ourselves.

To know Jesus, the truth

Knowing someone makes that person a part of our lives—so much so that separation causes pain, as if we had lost a part of ourselves. Love makes us want to know the other person better—to have not just an intellectual knowledge but a personal knowledge. When the first disciples began to share the good news, they proclaimed their experience of the person of Jesus Christ, living, healing, saving, teaching. Dogmas came later, when disputes arose as to the interpretation of Scripture and the understanding of who Jesus was.

Dogmas have their importance, but they should never take the place of experiencing the mystery, of knowing Jesus the truth who revealed to us, in his words, actions, and person, the very life of God and God's plan for his people, God's kingdom. Jesus not only gave us God's Word, he is God's Word. The revelation of God in Jesus Christ is contained in Sacred Scripture and in the living Tradition of the Church, and is summarized in the Creed. Catechesis is rooted in these abundant sources.

What does that mean for us as catechists? If we are ministers of the Word, we ourselves need to be in touch with the Scriptures and Tradition. An ancient prayer form called *lectio divina* can help us penetrate the meaning of Scripture more profoundly. It can put us in touch with Jesus in a more personal way. *Lectio divina* can be practiced both by individuals and groups. It includes four steps: reading, meditating, prayer, and contemplation.

First, we place ourselves in a quiet environment, and try to put all distracting thoughts aside. We choose the passage we want to reflect on and read it slowly, savoring the words.

Next, we meditate on the passage, seeking the hidden truth of its message. Here it is often helpful to focus on a word(s) or phrase(s) that especially struck us as we read the text.

Third, prayer follows as a movement of the heart in response to the truth we discovered in the Scripture reading. We don't need to force the prayer, just be open to God's movement in our heart. Prayerful silence in itself is often the response.

The last step, contemplation, the enjoyment of God's presence, often flows from this prayer. It may last only for a moment, but is a wonderful gift from God.

To celebrate Jesus, the life
As we gradually come to know the mystery of the living Christ, we want to celebrate his presence among us, and to remember as a community the stupendous events of our redemption. In turn, these celebrations are a source of catechesis, of helping the baptized enter more fully into the mystery of Jesus Christ.

The sacramental signs of bread and wine, of water and oil, of gestures and rituals, point to the deeper reality of Christ's saving action, as he becomes our life in a very personal encounter. What does this mean for us as catechists?

In order to help others encounter Jesus through these signs and symbols, we ourselves need to experience their richness in a fuller way, with our internal and external senses as well as our faith. Reflect, for example, on Jesus' encounter with the Samaritan woman at the well (Jn 4:1–26) which centered on the theme of Jesus as the living water. Picture a fountain, a spring, or a running brook; dip your hands into a bowl of fresh water; bless yourself with water from a clear stream. Or meditate on the multiplication of the loaves and fishes (Jn 6:1-14) which was a sign that pointed to Jesus, the bread of life. Make some bread; buy a fresh loaf of bread (unsliced), and bless, break, and share it with family or friends.

Read the parable of the prodigal son (Lk 15:11–32). Have a family celebration of reconciliation, including the sharing of a blessing cup and a "feast" afterwards. Celebrating these passages, and many others, together with the signs they contain, can help you gain insight into the sacramental signs.

Of course, in the celebration of the Eucharist, we experience both word and signs. Liturgy is not just a source of catechesis—it is the source. Everything points to God's presence. Jesus is our bread of life, in the Word as well as in the Eucharist. Jesus is our peace as we offer each other the sign of peace. Jesus is our forgiveness as we express our sorrow in the penitential rite. We encounter Jesus as fully as did the Samaritan woman, the disciples, Mary Magdalene, and all who lived and walked and spoke with him.

If the liturgy is the source and summit of Christian life for every Christian, much more should it be for us catechists, who need to accompany others on the journey of initiation. This is not just an intellectual exercise; it touches the reality of our day-to-day living. The faith that we celebrate in the liturgy needs to permeate our thoughts and actions. And we bring our concerns, our good works, our struggles and disappointments and joys, to offer to God during the Eucharist, just as the people of Jesus' time brought their lives to him.

To live Jesus, the way

A little girl was visiting the great cathedrals with her family. As the guide explained an historic tomb nearby, the girl was staring at a large stained glass window through which the summer sun was streaming. Suddenly she asked, "Who are those people in the window?"

"Those are the saints," the guide replied.

That night, as she was preparing for bed, the girl told her mother, "I know who the saints are."

"Do you, dear? Who are they?" her mother asked.

"They're the people who let the light shine through."

Letting Christ's light shine through requires a journey of interior transformation, not just external conformity to some rules and practices. It's a matter of acquiring the attitudes of Jesus, attitudes we find in the gospels, especially in the beatitudes.

Jesus didn't come just to tell us about God. He came to show us God, to put us in touch with God in his own person. That's the reality of the incarnation: that God walked with us, spoke with us, ate with us, dreamed with us, in the person of Jesus. Isn't it easier to learn something when we're shown how it's done rather than just told how it's done? Especially when what we are learning is complex? That is what Jesus did for us. He showed us God's kind of love. Again, what does this mean for us as catechists? We are called to incarnate our faith daily, to be "living editions of the gospel" as one spiritual writer put it.

We live out our vocation to holiness in the day-to-day world of family, business, home, neighbor, and community. "Spirituality," a sage once said, "is awareness."…The spirituality of work encourages people to be aware of grace in the house that contains smelly sneakers and dirty laundry; grace in the office that contains too many piles of file folders; grace in the classroom that contains noisy students. The spirituality of work encourages people to look for God and respond to God amid daily chores, among family members, and in the community.

—William Droel,
Full-Time Christians: The Real Challenge from Vatican II

We bring all these experiences of grace to our ministry as catechists.

To contemplate the mystery of Jesus

What are your favorite gospel passages? Take the time to prayerfully reflect on and note the passages you turn to most often. These will tell you something about yourself, something God is telling you about yourself. For example, at one point in my life the gospel passages that spoke to me the most were those in which Jesus is the healer. During that time I felt the need for healing on many levels. I also felt a profound and insistent call to be a healing influence in the lives of others.

Children as well as adults have their favorite gospel stories. These can be a key to what the person is feeling and how she or he is relating to Jesus and to God.

Where and from whom did Jesus himself learn to pray? One day when I was leafing through the section on prayer in the *Catechism of the Catholic Church*, this passage caught my eye.

The Son of God...learns to pray from his mother, who kept all the great things the Almighty had done and treasured them in her heart. He learns to pray in the words and rhythms of the prayer of his people, in the synagogue at Nazareth and the Temple of Jerusalem. (#2599)

I have to confess, I hadn't thought much about it before. But Jesus was a boy, a teenager, a man of his own people, religious culture, and time. What a perfect model he is for us catechists and for those we teach. Sometimes we might think of prayer as something detached or apart from our culture and century. Instead these enrich our prayer.

A more important source for Jesus' prayer was his relationship with his Father. "Father, I thank you for having heard me. I knew

18

that you always hear me" (Jn 11:41–42). Jesus' prayer, as recorded in the gospel, expresses his oneness with the Father. The Catechism puts it this way:

> The whole prayer of Jesus is contained in this loving adherence of his human heart to the mystery of the will of the Father. (#2603)

Isn't this, after all, the essence of prayer, of our relationship with God—loving adherence to God's will?

When Jesus prays, he prays for himself as well as for others. He prays before the decisive moments of his own mission: at his baptism, during his forty days of fasting in the desert, on the night before he chose his apostles, at the beginning of his passion. His prayer is in tune with the Father's heart.

In the gospel we find that Jesus prays constantly for others: for his apostles, for those who come to him to be healed, for the crowds who gather to hear his words, for his closest friends. We can use his example as a source of catechesis. When we learn to pray with Jesus, we pray with the same sentiments he did: adoration, praise, thanksgiving, confidence, supplication, and awe at the Father's glory (*GDC*, #85). When we learn from Jesus how to pray, we are like his disciples. They saw Jesus at prayer and asked, "Lord, teach us to pray." And Jesus taught them the Our Father, which has been called the compendium of the gospel. The Lord's Prayer is a catechesis in itself.

> What I love most about this ministry is teaching my first graders to pray and to talk to God. I also love reading and talking about the gospel stories. I really love being a catechist, and feel very close to the Lord by doing his ministry.
> —Janice M. Clay,
> Holy Name Parish, West Roxbury, Massachusetts

19

- Reread the story "Sharing the fire." Like all parables, it has several levels of meaning. It can be read as just a story. You may read it a second time and apply it to your life. But you may also read it a third time, deep in your heart, letting the story reveal to you its inner depth. Write here what this story means to you.

_____

_____

_____

_____

- Each time you read a gospel story, make notes about the passage. Did you draw a lesson from it? Did it touch you on a deeper level?

_____

_____

_____

_____

- Continue with the reflection above. After a few weeks look at the most recent group of passages that you wrote about. Do you see a pattern in them? What is Jesus doing in these passages? Is he healer? teacher? model? As noted earlier in this chapter, this may indicate how you best relate to Jesus at this point in your spiritual life. It may also indicate what you are called to be for others, both within and outside of your ministry as catechist. What might this mean for you?

_____

_____

_____

- Which one of the gestures, symbols, or rituals used at Mass (e.g., breaking of the bread, sign of the cross, consecration of the bread) or in the celebration of another sacrament, appeals to you the most or has the most significance for you? Reflect on what it means to you. Write a prayer based on your reflection.

_____

_____

_____

_____

FOR YOUR PRAYER

Let these words lead you to prayer.

If then there is any encouragement in Christ, any consolation from love, any sharing in the Spirit, any compassion and sympathy, make my joy complete: be of the same mind, having the same love, being in full accord and of one mind....Let the same mind be in you that was in Christ Jesus, who, though he was in the form of God, did not regard equality with God as something to be exploited, but emptied himself, taking the form of a slave, being born in human likeness. And being found in human form, he humbled himself and became obedient to the point of death—even death on a cross.

—Philippians 2:1–2, 5–8

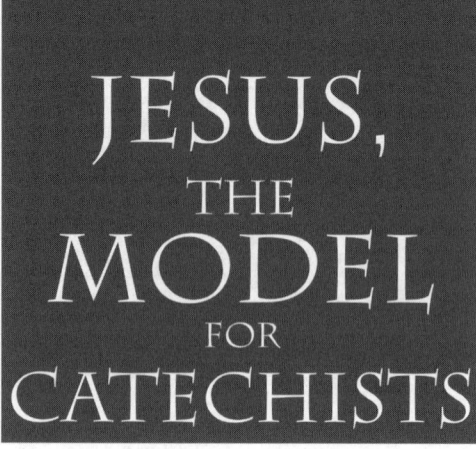

JESUS, THE MODEL FOR CATECHISTS

T he story is told of a very old Chinaman who was busy in his orchard when the ruler of that district happened to pass by. "You are very old, surely," said the ruler.

"I have lived one hundred years," replied the old man.

"Indeed?" The ruler was impressed. "But are you not planting fruit trees?"

"I am," said the old man.

"My friend," murmured the ruler, "surely you do not hope to live long enough to gather the fruit from these saplings? And if not, why make your back ache?"

"It is as you say," the gardener replied. "But, sire, when I came into this world I found many good things awaiting me. I would like to think that when I pass on, there will be good things waiting for others."

The gardener felt connected with the persons who had gone before him and those who would come after. He had benefited from the wisdom and talents of others, and wanted to pass that on to future generations. I also see in that gardener the image of Jesus the teacher.

Jesus presented himself to his disciples as the only teacher. "Christ [is] the Teacher who reveals God to man and man to himself, the Teacher who saves, sanctifies and guides, who lives, who speaks, rouses, moves, redresses, judges, forgives, and goes with us day by day" (*CT*, #9). Jesus' life was a continual teaching.

What do we see when we look at Jesus the teacher? We see someone who received others as persons loved by God. Jesus listened, he blessed, he comforted, he healed. He especially welcomed the poor, little ones, and sinners. Passages such as Jesus blessing the little children (Mt 19:13ff), or healing the paralytic (Mt 9:2–8), can serve as a guide to us in our ministry. We can always refer to Jesus' example when we have to resolve a discipline problem or a difficulty in relating to others.

Throughout the gospels we find that Jesus invited everyone he met to a life of faith, hope, and love, without coercion but with the persuasion and grace of his truth and his example. Think, for example, of the effect on his disciples when Jesus washed their feet (Jn 13:3–8), or his compassionate treatment of the woman caught in adultery (Jn 8:1–11).

Jesus proclaimed the kingdom of God without compromise yet with respect for his people. He adapted his presentation to his audience using words, images, and stories they could relate to. But he always and continually communicated the good news of the truth and of the consolation of the Father (*GDC*, # 140).

We can learn from Jesus how to adapt the message to our "audience." One way is to know the people (children, teens, adults) to whom we minister, as well as the things they like to do, to read, to watch, to play. This will enable us to use their language, and present the good news in a way that helps them enter the mystery of Jesus. We need to focus on those to whom we minister. We may have different approaches to setting and achieving goals, but the goals always need to be about the others—the children, teens, or adults we're teaching.

Jesus' love for his people was a delicate and strong love, a love that liberated them from evil and promoted life. He did not condone sin, neither did he condemn the sinner. His love allowed others to blossom.

In his teaching, Jesus employed the various resources of interpersonal communication: word, silence, metaphor, image, example, and sign. We will consider these in more detail later in this book.

FOR YOUR REFLECTION

•Are there some situations in which you have looked to Jesus' example for guidance? What are some of them?

_____

_____

_____

_____

•Read one of the following passages. What can you learn from it for your ministry as catechist? Lk 15:1–7; Lk 8:40–48; Mk 10:13–16; Mt 15:32–39.

_____

_____

_____

_____

•Watch a few of the television programs geared to the age level you are teaching. What can you learn from them about the children/teens of today? How might you apply this in your teaching?

_____

_____

_____

_____

• How might you proclaim the kingdom of God without compromise yet with respect for those you teach?

_____

_____

_____

FOR YOUR PRAYER

Let these words lead you to prayer.

While Mary contemplated everything she had read and heard, she grew even more in faith, wisdom, and charity. The mysteries of God were opened up to her, and joy filled her heart. Her mind was entirely blessed because, through the presence and action of the Spirit, she was always open to the power of God's word.

Do as Mary did. Look deep into your heart so you can be cleansed from your sins. Whether we contemplate the greatness of God or serve the needs of our neighbors by good works, we do all this through the love of Christ. We offer God our spiritual purification not in temples made by man but in the recesses of the heart where Jesus freely enters.

—St. Lawrence Justinian,
Sermon on the purification of the Blessed Virgin Mary

FORMATION
AND
QUALITIES
OF THE
CATECHIST

An eastern spiritual leader once said, "When I was a young man, I was a revolutionary. All my prayer to God was: 'Lord, give me the energy to change the world.'

"As I approached middle age, I realized that half my life was gone without my changing a single person. I changed my prayer to: 'Lord, give me the grace to change all those who come into contact with me. Just my family and friends, and I shall be satisfied.'

"Now that I am an old man and my days are numbered, I have begun to see how foolish I have been. My one prayer now is: 'Lord, give me the grace to change myself.' If I had prayed for this right from the start, I would not have wasted my life."

Allowing ourselves to be formed/transformed for the mission we are called to requires openness to the Spirit. The *General Directory for Catechesis* gives great importance to the formation of catechists. "The instruments provided for catechesis cannot be truly effective unless well used by trained catechists. Thus the adequate formation of catechists cannot be overlooked" (*GDC*, #234). This formation has different dimensions which can be summed up as being, knowing, and what the *GDC* calls *savoir faire*, the ability to communicate effectively (#238).

Catechists must first of all be witnesses, for, as Pope Paul VI wrote in *On Evangelization in the Modern World*, "the present century thirsts for authenticity" (*EN*, #76). Catechesis is effective only if it springs from true holiness of life, which is nourished by prayer and love for the Eucharist. This holiness, however, is not something achieved all at one moment, nor is it the result of our own efforts. It is a gift from God to us when we ready our hearts and seek God above all else (Mt 6:33). Formation nourishes the spirituality of the catechist.

The document *Guide for Catechists* stresses the importance of a deep spiritual life in the formation of catechists. "Spiritual formation should be a process of listening 'to him who is the principle inspiring all catechetical work and all who do this work—the Spirit of the Father and of the Son, the Holy Spirit'" (#22).

The following practices are recommended as key elements in the catechist's prayer life:

- Regular, even daily, reception of the Eucharist so as to nourish ourselves with the bread of life;
- A liturgy lived in its various dimensions;
- Recital of part of the Divine Office (the Liturgy of the Hours);
- Daily meditation, especially on the word of God;
- Personal prayer;
- Frequent celebration of the sacrament of penance;
- Participation in spiritual retreats.

The formation of catechists needs to ensure that catechists have an adequate knowledge of the message they are called to transmit and the people to whom they transmit it. Doctrinal formation is drawn from the following sources, most of which I have already talked about: the Scriptures, the history of the Church, the Creed, the liturgy, morality, and prayer. In addition, says the *GDC*, catechists need to have some knowledge of the basics of psychology and the social sciences to better understand the people to whom they minister.

But don't be overwhelmed. This doesn't necessarily mean only formal classes. Knowledge of people, as I mentioned earlier, can also be gained by studying what they are interested in. There are also books that provide simple explanations of the development and needs of children at different ages.

Effective Communication
Finally, because catechists are educators, ministers of the Word, they need to know how to communicate effectively. This involves learning techniques and methods that will facilitate growth in the experience of faith. Catechists can also learn this pedagogy by the way they themselves are instructed, and by self-formation through reading and observation.

As with any vocation, a person who feels called to be a catechist will want to discern whether he or she has the qualities needed to be an effective catechist. We'll reflect on some of these and how to develop them more fully.

The first quality mentioned by the *GDC* is a "deep faith" (#237). This means more than being able to list the Ten Commandments or recite the Creed. Having deep faith means that the catechist's life is centered in God in a relationship that permeates his or her words and actions. Of course, growing in faith is the journey of a lifetime. As we have seen, we develop and deepen our faith through a solid prayer life; frequent reflection on the Scriptures; and practice of the virtues of faith, hope, and love.

Catechists also need to have a "clear Christian and ecclesial identity," that is, they are to be truly and fully committed to Jesus Christ and to the Church. Ministers of the Word, catechists are called to proclaim Christ's message as presented by the Church's teaching authority. Familiarity with key Church documents, especially those relating to the catechetical ministry, is necessary to be in touch with the Church's position on important issues.

A third quality noted by the *GDC* is a "great social sensitivity." Those of us called to the catechetical ministry need to be aware not only of the sociological, economical, and cultural situation of the persons we minister to but also of the social justice issues that call us to prayer and action.

Catholic social teaching is an important part of our catechesis. We can read or watch the news not just to keep informed but prayerfully, to increase our awareness and concern for others. Pope Paul VI speaks of the love that should fill those who proclaim the Word. "It is much more than that of a teacher; it is the love of a father and of a mother. A sign of love will be the concern to give the truth and to bring people into unity" (*EN*, #79).

- Choose an area of catechesis with which you are least familiar: Scripture, Church history, the Creed, liturgy, morality, forms of prayer, or Catholic social teaching. What questions might you ask your priest or DRE about this area?

_____

_____

_____

_____

- Which of the key elements recommended by the *Guide for Catechists* do you already practice? How do they help you grow in your spiritual life?

_____

_____

_____

_____

- What gifts and talents do you bring to your ministry? How can you make the most of them? How might you turn weaknesses and obstacles into stepping stones?

_____

_____

_____

_____

- In what ways are you a "sign of love" to those you
  teach?

_____

_____

_____

_____

Let these words lead you to prayer.

Dear Jesus, help me to spread your fragrance everywhere.
Shine through me and be with me so that every person I
come in contact with may feel your presence in me. Let
them look up and see no longer me, but only Jesus.

—John Cardinal Newman

TOOLS
OF THE
TRADE

Whether you've been a catechist for twenty years or two, there are certain tools you will find helpful and necessary. One of these is lesson planning.

Planning with creativity

Have you ever noticed the different approaches you and other catechists take to lesson planning? Some of these differences might be expressed in such phrases as:

- Why a lesson plan? I rely on inspiration, on the question of the moment.

- My lesson plans are complete and structured down to the last dot on the last "i."

- I like to let ideas germinate for a while. I read each lesson ahead of time, then go about my daily tasks, open to inspiration and resources.

- I work with deadlines. I set my goals and force myself to come up with creative ideas.

- My lessons have to be filled with activities, high tech gadgets and gimmicks, to compete with the media for the children's attention.

- High tech entertainment isn't the answer and isn't within the reach of our budget. I like to give children time to talk about their needs and questions and to let them use their own imagination.

Any of these sound familiar? These differences are not irreconcilable. Actually these opposites can be brought together to form a balanced, effective approach to lesson planning, one that takes both details and creativity into account. (If you work with teens or adults, substitute the appropriate term in place of "children.")

- By all means focus on a goal for your lesson and flesh out the way to reach it. But as you teach, listen to the children and to the Scriptures. Let the lesson speak to them and their needs. And if a topic arises that is too important to ignore, adapt and structure your lesson around it.

- Set a schedule and goals and objectives for yourself, but include in that schedule time for relaxed, creative reflection (listening to music, stargazing, sitting in a park...).

- Brainstorm for ways to capture the children's imagination and attention quickly, and to hold them with the resources you have at hand. Then you can lead them into real-life situations and applications of the lessons to their own lives and in their language.

Lesson planning also includes personal preparation.

Occasionally observe yourself in a mirror. You might even ask someone you trust to watch you and offer their insights on your teaching approach and presentation.

Evaluation

Another tool that goes along with planning is evaluation. Evaluation allows you to recognize which elements work in your lesson plans and which are not as effective. Used wisely evaluation helps you grow and develop your gifts in different directions.

Here are some questions that can guide you in evaluating your lesson plan.

- Have I focused on the children?
- Have I concentrated on my goals and on the main point or points?
- Have I allowed room for spontaneity and the action of the Spirit? Am I ready to share my faith with the children?
- Have I planned for prayer time?
- Have I tried to plan according to my own teaching situation, taking into account the needs of my youngsters and events in our parish and neighborhood?
- What audio and visual aids have I planned to use (music, video, stories, textbook illustrations, etc.) to capture and hold the children's attention and to communicate the message?
- And most importantly: is Jesus the center of the message and method of this lesson? Will this lesson help the children grow in their relationship with him?

Other tools

Organizational tools can also make your ministry (and life) easier! A supplies box is a good way of keeping together the materials you need for your religion sessions. Preparing your learning environment ahead of time whenever possible (including equipment you will need) is important.

An effective tool that we often overlook is our own presence and attitude in the classroom. Using these well will help us communicate better and avoid or lessen discipline problems. For example, rather than remain seated at the desk or stand rooted in one spot, it's helpful to move around the meeting space. Such movement keeps the lesson and alive and keeps us in touch with those we are teaching.

Eye contact with our "audience" is another means of keeping communication alive and personal.

Patience and a sense of humor are invaluable qualities. Our sessions can be celebrations of faith if we season them with understanding and fun.

Learning how to make the best use of our texts and manuals, as well as visuals such as posters, material objects, games, videos, and more, is another key tool. See the section, Teaching as Jesus Did, for some ideas.

One further tool is collaboration. Sharing ideas with your catechetical leader and with other catechists is invaluable for helping you develop your skills, techniques, and method. It also provides support in moments of discouragement and difficulty. Communication with families is also an essential aspect of your ministry. More and more faith formation programs are recognizing the necessity and value of involving families, and indeed, the whole parish, in the catechetical process.

- How does lesson planning work for you? How often do you evaluate your lessons?

_____

_____

_____

_____

- Write down the tools that you use most often. What has your experience of collaboration been like?

_____

_____

_____

_____

- How do you involve families in your faith formation program? What challenges have you faced? Has it enriched your catechesis?

_____

_____

_____

_____

- What has given you the most joy in your role as catechist so far?

_____

_____

_____

_____

Let these words lead you to prayer.

Rejoice in Christ the teacher
Whose simple words, spoken so long ago,
Have opened worlds of discovery ever since.
Rejoice in the Spirit,
who plants in us a hunger for growth
that keeps us reaching after truth our whole lives long.
Rejoice in God the Creator
whose world is full of wonders
to amaze and delight us at every turn.
Rejoice in the gift of learning, the gift of helping others learn,
and, in rejoicing, know God's joy in you.

—Roberta Rominger,
600 Blessings and Prayers from Around the World

TEACHING AS JESUS DID

W e can learn from Jesus not only the content of what we teach and how to live it, but also some effective means for teaching. As the *GDC* points out, Jesus had "recourse to the resources of interpersonal communication: word, silence, metaphor, image, example, and sign" (*GDC*, #140). While these resources may take on new forms in our time, they are as engaging as ever. We can employ each and all of them to help others discover Jesus' presence in their lives: to know, to celebrate, to live, and to contemplate the mystery of Jesus.

To know

Jesus used words in many ways: to explain, to forgive, to call his disciples. He also was a great storyteller, and knew how to draw striking word pictures and comparisons, or choose an image to communicate a truth.

The parables of Jesus, for example—how much more appealing and memorable they are than a dry explanation. And more, parables are art forms. Sr. Carole Marie Kelly compares them to paintings. Like all art forms they have unlimited potential to touch each person individually. They must be "swallowed whole, absorbed by our whole being" because they engage the whole person and refer to the totality of the kingdom. "The kingdom of God is among you!" (Lk 17:21). A parable is not just a story with a moral lesson; it reveals hidden mysteries that are beyond words (Carole Marie Kelly, *A Handful of Fire: Praying Contemplatively with Scripture*).

Stories and storytelling are as old as the human race, but are often neglected in catechesis. Sacred Scripture is filled with stories of faith that were handed down for generations. But as Diane Crehan writes,

> ...somewhere along the way in our Catholic tradition, we have put aside the story of God's great love for us and focused on the creeds, formulas, and doctrines. Don't get me wrong; we still need to teach our creeds and doctrines. They are part of our church heritage. But I say we only have so much time to teach....So I say, first and foremost, tell the story!
> —*I Remember Jesus: Stories to Tell and How to Tell Them*

Metaphors and Images

Jesus also used metaphors and images to communicate a truth. Among the metaphors he used were: "you are the salt of the earth"; "I am the true vine"; "the eye is the lamp of the body"; and "I am the good shepherd." The gospels are full of images, whether they're found in stories or in references to the elements around Jesus; for example, the birds of the air, the flowers of the field, the grain of wheat, the sower, the treasure in the field. Of course, with today's technology we have many more types of images available to us: the textbooks, audio-visuals, computer programs, the Internet. One means that we perhaps don't make enough use of is our environment—both inside and outside our meeting space. What if we took more time in our religion sessions to explore the wonders of nature? What if we were able to design our meeting space according to a theme that was fun for the children we teach and a good vehicle for faith-sharing?

Another of Jesus' teaching methods related to words was his silence. In the gospels we find examples of different times of silence: times of retreat and prayer (Mt 14:13, 23; Mk 6:30, 46); important moments in Jesus' life (his baptism, transfiguration, and crucifixion); and the times when he listened to others (Jn 4:1-26; Lk 9:57-62; Lk 11:1–4). Listening is an important skill. We can learn from the persons to whom we minister—to learn their needs, their beliefs, their dreams, and how best to accompany them on their faith journey.

To live

Jesus used examples, first of all his own, to show his people the truth about God and the kingdom of God. He also pointed to the example of others: the widow putting the mite into the temple treasury; the centurion who expressed his faith in Jesus; the woman who anointed his feet.

Like Jesus we teach first of all through our own example. But we also have a wealth of examples in the lives of the saints and other Christian witnesses. We can share these examples through stories, visuals, drama, puppets, and so on.

We rely, too, on the example of the faith community, who also accompany those we catechize on their faith journey. Learning to be part of the community is an essential aspect of faith formation.

> Christian life is not realized spontaneously. It is necessary to educate it carefully. In this apprenticeship, the teaching of Christ on community life, recounted in the Gospel of St. Matthew, calls for attitudes which it is for catechesis to inculcate: the spirit of simplicity and humility...solicitude for the least among the brethren...common prayer...

mutual forgiveness. Fraternal love embraces all these attitudes. (*GDC*, #86)

To celebrate

Signs were an important part of Jesus' ministry. Through signs he showed his love for children (Mt 19:13); confirmed people's faith (Mk 7:24-30); answered the prayer of the suffering (Mk 7:31–37); forgave sin (Lk 5:17–26); and fed the hungry (Jn 6:1–15).

Signs are integral to our Catholic faith, especially the signs used in the liturgy: bread and wine, water, oil, signing with the cross, the altar, candles, incense, and more. Rituals and gestures involve us much more in the experience of mystery than mere words can. Using adaptations of the rites and rituals in our faith formation sessions is an excellent and necessary part of catechesis, of helping others discover the presence of Jesus in their lives. It is also effective in helping those we minister to enter into the mystery of the liturgical celebrations. For example, if you are presenting a session on baptism, you could use the ritual of blessing with water. During Lent you might have a ritual in which you present the cross to the children or adults in your group. Signs and gestures can definitely enrich your proclamation of God's Word.

Learning the Signs

We also need to learn the positive signs, symbols, and gestures that are part of our popular culture. These can give us a key as to how best to help others experience religious symbols and rituals. For example, why is a popular game or song or story character popular with children? If we can understand elements like that, we can use the same appeal to lead children to encounter Jesus.

To those of us committed to the catechetical ministry, Jesus says, "Do not be afraid; I am with you. Learn from me." Knowing that we can always turn to Christ the Teacher for inspiration and grace to carry out our work well enables us to make this journey of faith with confidence and love. Then we can say with St. Paul,

When I came to you, brothers and sisters, I did not come proclaiming the mystery of God to you in lofty words or wisdom. For I decided to know nothing among you except Jesus Christ, and him crucified.... My speech and my proclamation were not with plausible words of wisdom, but with a demonstration of the Spirit and of power, so that your faith might rest not on human wisdom but on the power of God.

—1 Corinthians 2:1–2, 4–5

FOR YOUR REFLECTION

• How do you employ storytelling in your faith formation sessions? You might share stories from Scripture, contemporary stories that teach moral values, or your own faith stories. Jot down some ideas for your next planning session.

_____

_____

_____

_____

• What kinds of images do you have available to you? How often do you make use of each of them? Do you use them, not as an end in themselves, but as a means to discover hidden truths?

_____

_____

_____

_____

- How well do you listen? Do you set aside some moments of silence in each lesson plan? What might you do to improve your listening skills?

_____

_____

_____

_____

- Those you teach look to you as a model of the way a Christian should live. Make a checklist of your strengths and weaknesses. Ask God's help in using your strengths and in turning your weaknesses into stepping stones on your faith journey.

_____

_____

_____

_____

_____

- What are some concrete ways you can make more use of signs, gestures, and rituals in your faith formation sessions?

_____

_____

_____

_____

_____

_____

_____

Let these words lead you to prayer.

If Christ dwells in us as our friend and leader, then we can bear all things, for he will help us, strengthen us, and never abandon us. Jesus is a true friend. If we desire to please God and be filled with his graces, these graces must come to us from Jesus' hands. What more do we desire from such a good friend? Happy the one who truly loves Jesus and remains at his side.

St. Teresa of Avila,
Autobiography

RESOURCES FOR FURTHER READING

- The General Directory for Catechesis in Plain English
  Bill Huebsch, 120 pp, $9.95

- A Prayerbook for Catechists
  Gwen Costello, 48 pp, $5.95

- Tools for Teaching: Classroom Tips for Catechists
  Joe Paprocki, 128 pp, $7.95

- Catholic Customs and Traditions: A Popular Guide
  Greg Dues, 224 pp, $9.95

- Basics of the Catholic Faith
  Bill, Patty & Lisa Coleman, 144 pp, $7.95

- A Prayer Primer for Catechists and Teachers
  Gwen Costello, 64 pp, $5.95

- What Would Jesus Do? A Catechist's Guide to Discipline
  Sr. Maxine Inkel, 112 pp, $10.95

- My Favorite Jesus Activity Book
  Jenny Erickson, 112 pp, 8 1/2 x11, $14.95

- Seven Steps to Great Religion Classes
  Joe Paprocki & Gwen Costello, 80 pp, $7.95

- Way of the Cross for Religion Teachers
  Gwen Costello, 32 pp, $1.95

- Teaching Is Like... Peeling Back Eggshells
  Sr. Melannie Svoboda, 120 pp, $7.95

- Jesus, I'm a Teacher Too
  Sr. Melannie Svoboda, 144 pp, $9.95

- 100 Fun Ways to Livelier Lessons
  Sr. Maxine Inkel, 128 pp, 81/2x11, $14.95

- School-Year Activities for Religion Classes
  Gwen Costello, 64 pp, $7.95

All of these resources are available from;

Twenty-Third Publications
A DIVISION OF BAYARD
185 Willow Street • P.O. Box 180
Mystic, CT 06355
(860) 536-2611 • (800) 321-0411
www.twentythirdpublications.com

PRAYER
FOR
CATECHISTS

Blessed Mother Mary and all you angels and saints of God, I join my voice to yours this day as I praise and thank God for the many blessings in my life. Help me to be grateful for my call to be a catechist and for all the good things that happen as I proclaim God's holy Word. May I be open to the many small surprises that God places in my path today. May I have the courage to teach what is right and to put the needs and concerns of those I teach before my own. Surround me and challenge me this day to do all that God asks of me. Amen.